SO-AFX-835

Beetles

by Cheryl Coughlan

goldsmith beetle

Consulting Editor: Gail Saunders-Smith, Ph.D.

Consultant: Gary A. Dunn, Director of Education,
Young Entomologists' Society

Pebble Books

an imprint of Capstone Press
Mankato, Minnesota

Pebble Books are published by Capstone Press
151 Good Counsel Drive, P.O. Box 669, Mankato, Minnesota 56002
http://www.capstone-press.com

Copyright © 1999 Capstone Press. All rights reserved.
No part of this publication may be reproduced in whole or in part, or stored in a
retrieval system, or transmitted in any form or by any means, electronic, mechanical,
photocopying, recording, or otherwise, without written permission of the publisher.
For information regarding permission, write to Capstone Press,
151 Good Counsel Drive, P.O. Box 669, Dept. R, Mankato, Minnesota 56002.
Printed in the United States of America

2 3 4 5 6 7 08 07 06 05 04 03

Library of Congress Cataloging-in-Publication Data
Coughlan, Cheryl.
    Beetles / by Cheryl Coughlan.
    p. cm.—(Insects)
    Summary: Photographs and simple text depict the features and behavior
of beetles.
    ISBN 0-7368-0235-5 (hardcover)
    ISBN 0-7368-4880-0 (paperback)
    1. Beetles—Juvenile literature. [1. Beetles.] I. Title. II. Series.
QL576.2.C68 1999
595.76—dc21   98-52996

Note to Parents and Teachers

The Insects series supports national science standards for units on
the diversity and unity of life. The series shows that animals have
features that help them live in different environments. This book
describes and illustrates the parts of beetles. The photographs
support early readers in understanding the text. The repetition of
words and phrases helps early readers learn new words. This book
also introduces early readers to subject-specific vocabulary words,
which are defined in the Words to Know section. Early readers may
need assistance to read some words and to use the Table of
Contents, Words to Know, Read More, Internet Sites, and
Index/Word List sections of the book.

Table of Contents

Beetles 5
Legs and Wings 11
Jaws and Eating 17

Words to Know 22
Read More 23
Internet Sites 23
Index/Word List 24

Beetles can be
many colors.

six-spotted tiger beetle

6

Some beetles are small.

mealworm beetle

Some beetles are big.

female rhinoceros beetle

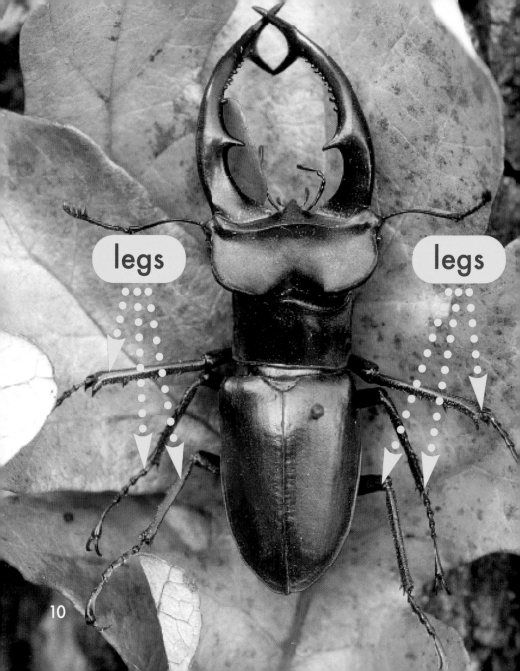

legs

legs

Beetles have six legs.

giant stag beetle

hard wings

Beetles have
two hard wings.

golden net-wing beetle

soft wings

Beetles have
two soft wings.

longhorn beetle

jaws

Beetles have strong jaws.

reddish-brown stag beetle

Some beetles eat plants.

glorious June beetle

20

Some beetles eat insects.

fiery searcher beetle eating
gypsy moth caterpillar

Words to Know

insect—a small animal with a hard outer shell, three body parts, six legs, and two antennas; insects may have two or four wings.

jaw—a mouthpart used to grab things, bite, and chew; beetles' jaws move from side to side when they chew.

wing—a movable part of an insect that helps it fly; a beetle has hard front wings that cover soft back wings; the hard wings are called elytra and are not used for flying.

Read More

Gerholdt, James E. *Beetles.* Incredible Insects. Edina, Minn.: Abdo and Daughters, 1996.

Julivert, Maria Ángels. *The Fascinating World of Beetles.* Hauppauge, N.Y.: Barron's, 1995.

Stefoff, Rebecca. *Beetle.* Living Things. New York: Benchmark Books/Marshall Cavendish, 1997.

Internet Sites

Visit the FactHound at *http://www.facthound.com*

Here's how:

1) Visit the **FactHound** home page.

2) Enter a search word or type in this code: **0736802355**

3) Click on the **Fetch It** button.

Your trusty friend FactHound will fetch the best site for you!

Index/Word List

beetles, 5, 7, 9, 11,
  13, 15, 17, 19, 21
big, 9
colors, 5
eat, 19, 21
hard, 13
insects, 21
jaws, 17
legs, 11

many, 5
plants, 19
six, 11
small, 7
soft, 15
some, 7, 9, 19, 21
strong, 17
two, 13, 15
wings, 13, 15

Word Count: 39
Early-Intervention Level: 6

Editorial Credits

Martha E. Hillman, editor; Timothy Halldin, cover designer; Kimberly Danger,
    photo researcher

Photo Credits

Bill Johnson, 16
Connie Toops, 6
David Liebman, cover, 4, 10, 18
James P. Rowan, 1
Rob and Ann Simpson, 8, 20
Rob Curtis, 12, 14